# SMALL BATCH BAKING FOR ONE GUIDE

### 25 Sweet and Appetizing Delicious Bakes to Satisfy Your Cravings

RACHEL OBERLE

Copyright © 2023 by RACHEL OBERLE

All rights reserved. No part of this publication may be reproduced, distributed, or transmitted in any form or by any means, including photocopying, recording, or other electronic or mechanical methods, without the prior written permission of the publisher, except in the case of brief quotations embodied in critical reviews and certain other non-commercial uses permitted by copyright law.

# TABLE OF CONTENTS

INTRODUCTION

25 RECIPES FOR SMALL-SIZED BAKING PORTIONS

RECIPE 1: CHOCOLATE CHIP COOKIES

RECIPE 2: BLUEBERRY MUFFINS

RECIPE 3: MINI CHEESECAKE

RECIPE 4: PEANUT BUTTER ENERGY BALLS

RECIPE 5: SINGLE-SERVE BROWNIE

RECIPE 6: INDIVIDUAL APPLE CRISP

RECIPE 7: MINI QUICHE

RECIPE 8: SINGLE-SERVING BANANA BREAD

RECIPE 9: PERSONAL-SIZED PIZZA

RECIPE 10: INDIVIDUAL LEMON BARS

RECIPE 11: MINI FRITTATA

RECIPE 12: SINGLE-SERVING CINNAMON ROLL

RECIPE 13: MINI CORNBREAD MUFFIN

RECIPE 14: PERSONAL-SIZED OMELETTE

RECIPE 15: MINI BANANA PANCAKES

RECIPE 16: INDIVIDUAL CRUSTLESS QUICHE

RECIPE 17: MINI PUMPKIN BREAD

RECIPE 18: INDIVIDUAL BERRY CRUMBLE

RECIPE 19: MINI LEMON POPPY SEED MUFFIN

RECIPE 20: PERSONAL-SIZED ZUCCHINI BREAD

RECIPE 21: MINI CARAMELIZED ONION AND GOAT CHEESE TART

RECIPE 22: MINI VEGETABLE LASAGNA

RECIPE 23: INDIVIDUAL APPLE GALETTE

RECIPE 24: MINI CAPRESE SKEWERS

RECIPE 25: SINGLE-SERVING CINNAMON APPLE CRISP

CONCLUSION

# INTRODUCTION

In a bustling city, a young professional named Emily sought a solution to her busy lifestyle that often left little time for cooking. She discovered the benefits of small batch baking for one recipes, and it revolutionized her approach to meal preparation.

The advantages were plentiful. Firstly, these recipes provided quick and easy meals that could be made in a fraction of the time required for traditional cooking. With just a few simple ingredients and minimal effort, Emily could create delicious and satisfying dishes.

Furthermore, small batch baking allowed Emily to control portion sizes, avoiding food waste and promoting healthier eating habits. She no longer had to contend with an excess of leftovers that often went uneaten.

Not only did small batch baking provide practical benefits, but it also sparked Emily's creativity in the kitchen. She experimented with a variety of flavors and ingredients, discovering unique combinations that delighted her taste buds.

In the end, small batch baking proved to be a game-changer for Emily, allowing her to enjoy quick, easy, and delectable meals while maintaining a balanced and efficient lifestyle.

# 25 RECIPES FOR SMALL-SIZED BAKING PORTIONS

## Recipe 1: Chocolate Chip Cookies

**Ingredients:**

1/4 cup all-purpose flour

2 tablespoons butter, softened

2 tablespoons brown sugar

1 tablespoon granulated sugar

1/4 teaspoon vanilla extract

1/8 teaspoon baking soda

Pinch of salt

2 tablespoons chocolate chips

**Procedure:**

1. Set the oven's temperature to 350°F (175°C).
2. Cream the softened butter, brown sugar, and granulated sugar in a bowl.
3. Mix thoroughly after adding the vanilla extract.
4. Combine the flour, baking soda, and salt in a separate basin.
5. The dry ingredients should be added gradually to the butter mixture and mixed thoroughly.
6. Add the chocolate chunks and stir.
7. The dough should be formed into little balls, which you should then arrange on a parchment-lined baking sheet.
8. Until the rims are golden brown, bake for 8 to 10 minutes.
9. Before moving the cookies to a wire rack, give them some time to cool on the baking sheet.

## *Recipe 2: Blueberry Muffins*

**Ingredients:**

1/4 cup all-purpose flour

2 tablespoons sugar

1/4 teaspoon baking powder

Pinch of salt

2 tablespoons milk

1 tablespoon vegetable oil

1/4 teaspoon vanilla extract

2 tablespoons fresh or frozen blueberries

**Procedure:**

1. Set the oven's temperature to 375°F (190°C).
2. Mix the flour, sugar, baking soda, and salt in a bowl.
3. Mix just till incorporated after adding the milk, vegetable oil, and vanilla essence to the dry ingredients.
4. Fold the blueberries in slowly.
5. Use paper liners or pour the batter into a muffin pan that has been buttered.
6. A toothpick inserted in the center of the cake should come out clean after baking for 15 to 18 minutes.
7. Before moving the muffins to a wire rack, give them a few minutes to cool in the pan.

## Recipe 3: Mini Cheesecake

**Ingredients:**

2 tablespoons graham cracker crumbs

2 tablespoons cream cheese, softened

1 tablespoon sugar

1/4 teaspoon vanilla extract

1 egg

**Procedure:**

1. Set the oven's temperature to 325°F (160°C).
2. In the bottom of a ramekin or small baking dish that has been buttered, evenly distribute the graham cracker crumbs.
3. Cream cheese should be well beaten in a bowl.
4. Mix the cream cheese well with the sugar and vanilla essence.
5. Egg should be properly included after being added.
6. The graham cracker crumbs in the ramekin should be covered with the cream cheese mixture.
7. Bake the cheesecake for 15 to 20 minutes, or until it is firm.
8. Before chilling it for at least an hour, let it cool.

## Recipe 4: Peanut Butter Energy Balls

**Ingredients:**

2 tablespoons peanut butter

1 tablespoon honey

2 tablespoons rolled oats

1 tablespoon shredded coconut

1 tablespoon mini chocolate chips

**Procedure:**

1. The peanut butter and honey should be thoroughly combined in a bowl.
2. To the bowl, add the rolled oats, coconut shreds, and small chocolate chips. Combine well.
3. Using the ingredients, form little balls.
4. Before serving, place the energy balls on a dish and chill for at least 30 minutes.

## Recipe 5: Single-Serve Brownie

**Ingredients:**

2 tablespoons butter

2 tablespoons sugar

1 tablespoon cocoa powder

1/4 teaspoon vanilla extract

1 egg

2 tablespoons all-purpose flour

Pinch of salt

**Procedure:**

1. Set the oven's temperature to 350°F (175°C).
2. Melt the butter in a dish that can go in the microwave.
3. The sugar, cocoa powder, and vanilla extract should all be thoroughly mixed in.
4. Mix in the egg completely after adding it.
5. Add salt and flour by blending.
6. Fill a greased ramekin or small baking dish with the batter.
7. A toothpick inserted into the center should come out with a few wet crumbs after baking for 12 to 15 minutes.
8. Before serving, let the brownies cool somewhat.

# Recipe 6: Individual Apple Crisp

**Ingredients:**

1 small apple, peeled and thinly sliced

1 tablespoon brown sugar

1 tablespoon all-purpose flour

1 tablespoon rolled oats

1 tablespoon butter, softened

1/4 teaspoon cinnamon

**Procedure:**

1. Set the oven's temperature to 375°F (190°C).
2. Sliced apple, brown sugar, flour, rolled oats, softened butter, and cinnamon are all combined in a bowl.
3. Mix until the mixture is evenly distributed over the apples.

4. Place the apple mixture in a ramekin or small baking dish that has been buttered.
5. Bake for 20 to 25 minutes, or until the top is golden brown and the apples are soft.

6. Before serving, let the apple crisp cool just a little.

## *Recipe 7: Mini Quiche*

**Ingredients**:

1 egg

2 tablespoons milk

2 tablespoons shredded cheese

1 tablespoon chopped vegetables (such as spinach, bell peppers, or mushrooms)

Salt and pepper to taste

**Procedure:**

1. Set the oven's temperature to 375°F (190°C).
2. Whisk the egg and milk together in a bowl.
3. Add the salt, pepper, shredded cheese, and chopped veggies by stirring.
4. Put the mixture in a small baking dish or ramekin that has been buttered.
5. Bake the quiche for 15 to 20 minutes, or until it is set and the top is gently brown.
6. Before serving, let it cool a little.

# Recipe 8: Single-Serving Banana Bread

**Ingredients:**

1/2 ripe banana, mashed

2 tablespoons all-purpose flour

1 tablespoon sugar

1/4 teaspoon baking powder

1/8 teaspoon cinnamon

1 tablespoon milk

1/2 tablespoon vegetable oil

1/4 teaspoon vanilla extract

**Procedure:**

1. Set the oven's temperature to 350°F (175°C).
2. The mashed banana, flour, sugar, baking powder, and cinnamon should all be combined in a bowl.
3. Mix just till incorporated after adding the milk, vegetable oil, and vanilla essence to the bowl.
4. Fill a greased ramekin or small baking dish with the batter.
5. A toothpick placed in the center of the cake should come out clean after 20 to 25 minutes of baking.
6. Before serving, let the banana bread cool down.

## Recipe 9: Personal-Sized Pizza

**Ingredients:**

1 small pre-made pizza crust or pita bread

2 tablespoons pizza sauce

2 tablespoons shredded mozzarella cheese

Your choice of pizza toppings (such as pepperoni, mushrooms, onions, or bell peppers)

**Procedure:**

1. Set the oven's temperature to what your pizza crust requires.
2. On a baking sheet or pizza stone, place the pita bread or pizza dough.
3. Over the crust, evenly distribute the pizza sauce.
4. Over the sauce, strew mozzarella cheese crumbles.
5. Add the pizza toppings of your choice.
6. The pizza dough should be baked in accordance with the directions on the package, or until the cheese is melted and bubbling.
7. Before cutting and serving, let the pizza cool just a little.

## Recipe 10: Individual Lemon Bars

**Ingredients:**

For the crust:

2 tablespoons butter, softened

1 tablespoon sugar

4 tablespoons all-purpose flour

For the filling:

1 tablespoon lemon juice

1/2 teaspoon lemon zest

2 tablespoons sugar

1 tablespoon all-purpose flour

1 egg

**Procedure:**
1. Set the oven's temperature to 350°F (175°C).
2. Cream the sugar and softened butter in a bowl.
3. Add the flour little by little while mixing the mixture until it resembles crumbs.
4. In a ramekin or small baking dish that has been buttered, press the crust mixture into the bottom.

5. Lemon juice, lemon zest, sugar, flour, and egg should all be well blended in a separate basin.
6. Over the crust in the ramekin, pour the lemon filling.
7. Bake the filling for 15 to 18 minutes, or until it has set.
8. Before serving, let the lemon bars to cool.

## *Recipe 11: Mini Frittata*

**Ingredients:**

1 egg

2 tablespoons milk

1 tablespoon chopped vegetables (such as spinach, bell peppers, or onions)

1 tablespoon shredded cheese

Salt and pepper to taste

**Procedure:**

1. Set the oven's temperature to 375°F (190°C).
2. Whisk the egg and milk together in a bowl.

3. Add the shredded cheese, minced veggies, salt, and pepper.
4. Put the mixture in a small baking dish or ramekin that has been buttered.
5. The frittata should be baked for 12 to 15 minutes, or until set and gently browned on top.
6. Before serving, let it cool a little.

## *Recipe 12: Single-Serving Cinnamon Roll*

**Ingredients:**

For the dough:

1/4 cup all-purpose flour

1 tablespoon sugar

1/4 teaspoon baking powder

Pinch of salt

2 tablespoons milk

1/2 tablespoon vegetable oil

For the filling:

1 tablespoon butter, softened

1 tablespoon brown sugar

1/2 teaspoon ground cinnamon

For the glaze:

1 tablespoon powdered sugar

1/4 teaspoon milk

**Procedure:**

1. Set the oven's temperature to 375°F (190°C).
2. Mix the flour, sugar, baking soda, and salt in a bowl.
3. Mix the dry ingredients just enough to blend before adding the milk and vegetable oil.
4. For the filling, combine the softened butter, brown sugar, and cinnamon in a separate bowl.
5. The dough is rolled out into a thin rectangle.
6. Over the dough, distribute the filling mixture evenly.
7. To make a little cinnamon roll, tightly roll up the dough starting at one end.
8. Put the cinnamon roll in a small baking dish or ramekin that has been buttered.
9. Until golden brown, bake for 12 to 15 minutes.
10. The glaze is made by combining milk and powdered sugar in a small bowl.

11. Before serving, drizzle the glaze over the heated cinnamon roll.

## Recipe 13: Mini Cornbread Muffin

**Ingredients:**

2 tablespoons cornmeal

2 tablespoons all-purpose flour

1 tablespoon sugar

1/4 teaspoon baking powder

Pinch of salt

2 tablespoons milk

1 tablespoon vegetable oil

1/4 teaspoon honey

**Procedure:**

1. Set the oven's temperature to 375°F (190°C).
2. Cornmeal, flour, sugar, baking soda, and salt should all be combined in a bowl.
3. Mix the dry ingredients just enough to blend before adding the milk, vegetable oil, and honey.

4. Use paper liners or pour the batter into a tiny muffin pan that has been buttered.
5. Bake for 10 to 12 minutes, or until toothpick inserted in the center of the cake comes out clean and the top is golden brown.
6. Before transferring the cornbread muffins to a wire rack, let them cool in the pan for a few minutes.

## *Recipe 14: Personal-Sized Omelette*

**Ingredients:**

2 eggs

2 tablespoons milk

1 tablespoon chopped vegetables (such as spinach, bell peppers, or mushrooms)

1 tablespoon shredded cheese

Salt and pepper to taste

**Procedure:**

1. Set the oven's temperature to 375°F (190°C).
2. Combine the milk and eggs in a bowl.
3. Add the shredded cheese, minced veggies, salt, and pepper.

4. Put the mixture in a small baking dish or ramekin that has been buttered.
5. The omelette should be baked for 15 to 20 minutes, or until set and faintly browned on top.
6. Before serving, let it cool a little.

## Recipe 15: Mini Banana Pancakes

**Ingredients:**

2 tablespoons all-purpose flour

1/2 teaspoon sugar

1/4 teaspoon baking powder

Pinch of salt

2 tablespoons milk

1/2 tablespoon vegetable oil

1/4 teaspoon vanilla extract

1/2 ripe banana, mashed

**Procedure:**

1. Mix the flour, sugar, baking soda, and salt in a bowl.

2. Then combine the dry ingredients with the milk, vegetable oil, vanilla essence, and mashed banana.
3. A small nonstick pan should be heated to medium heat.
4. To create little pancakes, drop tiny dollops of the batter onto the pan.
5. Cook until golden brown, about one to two minutes per side.
6. You may top the little pancakes with your favorite ingredients, such maple syrup or fresh fruit.

## *Recipe 16: Individual Crustless Quiche*

**Ingredients:**

1 egg

2 tablespoons milk

1 tablespoon chopped vegetables (such as spinach, bell peppers, or onions)

1 tablespoon shredded cheese

Salt and pepper to taste

**Procedure:**

1. Set the oven's temperature to 375°F (190°C).

2. Whisk the egg and milk together in a bowl.
3. Add the shredded cheese, minced veggies, salt, and pepper.
4. Put the mixture in a small baking dish or ramekin that has been buttered.
5. Bake the quiche for 12 to 15 minutes, or until it is set and the top is gently brown.
6. Before serving, let it cool a little.

## *Recipe 17: Mini Pumpkin Bread*

**Ingredients:**

2 tablespoons canned pumpkin puree

2 tablespoons all-purpose flour

1 tablespoon sugar

1/4 teaspoon baking powder

1/8 teaspoon cinnamon

Pinch of nutmeg

Pinch of cloves

1 tablespoon milk

1/2 tablespoon vegetable oil

**Procedure:**

1. Set the oven's temperature to 350°F (175°C).
2. Pumpkin puree, flour, sugar, baking powder, cinnamon, nutmeg, and cloves should all be combined in a bowl.
3. Mix just till incorporated after adding the milk and vegetable oil to the basin.
4. Fill a greased ramekin or small baking dish with the batter.
5. A toothpick placed in the center of the cake should come out clean after 20 to 25 minutes of baking.
6. Before serving, let the pumpkin bread to cool.

## *Recipe 18: Individual Berry Crumble*

**Ingredients:**

For the filling:

1/4 cup mixed berries (such as strawberries, blueberries, and raspberries)

1 tablespoon sugar

1/2 teaspoon cornstarch

For the crumble topping:

2 tablespoons all-purpose flour

1 tablespoon rolled oats

1 tablespoon brown sugar

1 tablespoon butter, softened

Pinch of cinnamon

**Procedure:**

1. Set the oven's temperature to 375°F (190°C).
2. The filling's ingredients are mixed berries, sugar, and cornstarch in a small dish.
3. For the crumble topping, combine the flour, rolled oats, brown sugar, butter that has been melted, and cinnamon in a separate dish and stir until the mixture forms coarse crumbs.
4. Put the berry filling in a tiny baking dish or ramekin that has been buttered.
5. Over the berries, evenly distribute the crumble topping.
6. Bake the berries for 15 to 18 minutes, or until they are bubbling and the topping is browned.
7. Before serving, let the berry crumble cool just a bit.

### *Recipe 19: Mini Lemon Poppy Seed Muffin*

**Ingredients:**

2 tablespoons all-purpose flour

1 tablespoon sugar

1/4 teaspoon baking powder

Pinch of salt

1 tablespoon milk

1/2 tablespoon vegetable oil

1/2 teaspoon lemon zest

1/4 teaspoon lemon juice

1/2 teaspoon poppy seeds

**Procedure:**

1. Set the oven's temperature to 375°F (190°C).
2. Mix the flour, sugar, baking soda, and salt in a bowl.
3. To the dry ingredients, add the milk, vegetable oil, lemon zest, lemon juice, and poppy seeds. Combine everything together just until incorporated.
4. Use paper liners or pour the batter into a tiny muffin pan that has been buttered.
5. When a toothpick placed in the center of the cake comes out clean, bake for 10 to 12 minutes.
6. Before transferring the lemon poppy seed muffins to a wire rack, let them cool in the pan for a few minutes.

# Recipe 20: Personal-Sized Zucchini Bread

**Ingredients:**

2 tablespoons grated zucchini

2 tablespoons all-purpose flour

1 tablespoon sugar

1/4 teaspoon baking powder

1/8 teaspoon cinnamon

Pinch of salt

1 tablespoon milk

1/2 tablespoon vegetable oil

1/4 teaspoon vanilla extract

**Procedure:**

1. Set the oven's temperature to 350°F (175°C).
2. Grated zucchini, flour, sugar, baking powder, cinnamon, and salt should all be combined in a basin.

3. Mix just till incorporated after adding the milk, vegetable oil, and vanilla essence to the bowl.
4. Fill a greased ramekin or small baking dish with the batter.
5. A toothpick placed in the center of the cake should come out clean after 20 to 25 minutes of baking.
6. Before serving, let the zucchini bread cool down.

## *Recipe 21: Mini Caramelized Onion and Goat Cheese Tart*

**Ingredients:**

1/4 cup diced onion

1/2 tablespoon butter

1/2 tablespoon olive oil

1/2 tablespoon balsamic vinegar

1/2 tablespoon brown sugar

1 sheet of puff pastry, thawed

2 tablespoons crumbled goat cheese

Salt and pepper to taste

**Procedure:**

1. Set the oven's temperature to 400°F (200°C).
2. Melt the butter and olive oil in a pan over medium heat.
3. Stirring occasionally, add the chopped onion to the pan and heat until caramelized.
4. Cook for another minute after adding the brown sugar and balsamic vinegar.
5. The puff pastry sheet should be rolled out and cut into a little square or circle.
6. Puff pastry should be placed on a baking pan covered with parchment paper.
7. Over the puff pastry, evenly smear the caramelized onions.
8. On top, scatter the goat cheese crumbles.
9. Add salt and pepper to taste.
10. Bake the puff pastry for 15 to 20 minutes, or until golden brown.
11. Before serving, let the tart somewhat cool.

## Recipe 22: Mini Vegetable Lasagna

**Ingredients:**

2 lasagna noodles, cooked according to package instructions

2 tablespoons marinara sauce

1/4 cup chopped vegetables (such as zucchini, bell peppers, or mushrooms)

2 tablespoons ricotta cheese

2 tablespoons shredded mozzarella cheese

Salt and pepper to taste

**Procedure:**

1. Set the oven's temperature to 375°F (190°C).
2. One cooked lasagna noodle should be placed on a level surface.
3. The noodle should have 1 tablespoon of marinara sauce on it.
4. Distribute equally over the sauce the other half of the chopped veggies.
5. On top of the veggies, add 1 spoonful of ricotta cheese.
6. Over the ricotta, top with 1 tablespoon of mozzarella cheese shreds.
7. Add salt and pepper to taste.
8. The lasagna noodle should be tightly rolled before being put in a small baking dish or oiled ramekin.
9. With the second lasagna noodle, repeat steps 2 through 8.
10. Bake for 15 to 18 minutes, or until bubbling and melted cheese.
11. Before serving, let the little veggie lasagnas cool a little.

## *Recipe 23: Individual Apple Galette*

**Ingredients:**

1 small apple, thinly sliced

1 tablespoon sugar

1/4 teaspoon cinnamon

1/2 tablespoon butter, melted

1 sheet of puff pastry, thawed

1 tablespoon apricot jam (optional, for glaze)

**Procedure:**

1. Set the oven's temperature to 375°F (190°C).
2. Apple slices, sugar, cinnamon, and melted butter should all be combined in a bowl.
3. The puff pastry sheet should be rolled out and put on a parchment-lined baking pan.
4. Puff pastry should have a border around the edges, and the apple slices should be arranged in the center.
5. Puff pastry's edges are folded over the apples, partially encasing them.
6. **Optional:** In order to glaze the apples and pastry, microwave the apricot jam until it is warm.
7. Bake the crust for 25 to 30 minutes, or until golden brown and the apples are soft.
8. Before serving, let the apple galette cool just a little.

## Recipe 24: Mini Caprese Skewers

**Ingredients:**

4 cherry tomatoes, halved

4 mini mozzarella balls

4 small basil leaves

1/2 tablespoon balsamic glaze

Salt and pepper to taste

**Procedure:**

1. A toothpick or tiny skewer should be used to thread a cherry tomato half onto.
2. A little mozzarella ball should be placed on the skewer.
3. Top the mozzarella with a little basil leaf.
4. With the remaining ingredients, repeat steps 1-3.
5. Place the little caprese skewers on a dish for serving.
6. Balsamic glaze should be drizzled over the skewers.
7. Add salt and pepper to taste.
8. As a tasty starter or snack, serve.

# Recipe 25: Single-Serving Cinnamon Apple Crisp

**Ingredients:**

1 small apple, peeled, cored, and diced
1/2 tablespoon lemon juice
1/2 tablespoon sugar
1/4 teaspoon cinnamon
2 tablespoons rolled oats
1 tablespoon all-purpose flour
1 tablespoon brown sugar
1/2 tablespoon butter, softened

**Procedure:**

1. Set the oven's temperature to 375°F (190°C).
2. Diced apple should be well covered in a bowl after being mixed with sugar, cinnamon, and lemon juice.
3. For the crisp topping, mix the rolled oats, flour, brown sugar, and softened butter in a another bowl.
4. Put the apple mixture in a small baking dish or ramekin that has been buttered.

5. Spread the apples out with the crisp topping, evenly coating them.
6. Bake the topping for 20 to 25 minutes, or until golden brown and the apples are soft.
7. Before serving, let the apple crisp with cinnamon slightly cool.

*Please take note that these recipes are designed to feed one person. If you'd want to produce bigger batches, adjust the quantities appropriately.*

# CONCLUSION

In conclusion, the world of small batch baking for one has opened up a realm of possibilities for those seeking quick, easy, and delicious meals tailored to their individual needs. This guide has shed light on the numerous benefits of small batch baking, from efficient use of ingredients to portion control and reduced food waste.

Small batch baking empowers individuals to embark on culinary adventures, experimenting with flavors and creating meals that bring joy and satisfaction. It provides a pathway to explore creativity in the kitchen, allowing for customization and personalization of dishes.

Moreover, small batch baking is a practical solution for busy lifestyles, providing the convenience of preparing meals in a fraction of the time required for traditional cooking methods. It is a testament to the fact that delicious and wholesome meals can be achieved without sacrificing time or effort.

So, whether you are a solo dweller, a busy professional, or simply someone seeking culinary efficiency, embrace the world of small batch baking for one. Unleash your inner chef, savor the delights of homemade meals, and embark on a journey of culinary bliss tailored just for you.

Printed in Great Britain
by Amazon